Peter: Conversations With a Little White Dog

Once during your life, if you are lucky, you may have a heart dog. A dog whose wisdom, gentleness, love, and grace teaches you an enormous amount about life and death … and yourself. Ed Hickling was such a lucky man when he and his wife Linda adopted Peter, a Bichon Frise with a bad haircut. In this lovely book, Ed reflects on his relationship with Peter through a series of letters written to one another after Peter's death. Piercing the surface, these letters illustrate the depth of their bond. This book provides important guidance about love and loss. In a fast-paced world, it reminds the reader to slow down and appreciate what is right in front of them. Guideposts for facing difficult situations and emotions are woven throughout this book, rendering it helpful as a tool for mental health professionals in guiding clients through loss, grief, and pain. And if you have ever been lucky enough to have a heart dog, this book will touch the special place where you hold them.

> —*J. Gayle Beck, Ph.D., Chair of Excellence Emerita, Department of Psychology, The University of Memphis Trustee, American Psychological Foundation Member, Board of Scientific Affairs, American Psychological Association*

In *Peter: Conversations with a Little White Dog*, Ed Hickling penned a touching dialogue between himself and the family's "heart dog". The unconditional support of a dog became self-evident during a emergency hospital visit by Ed and his wife. When the family was gifted a sweet, small, "puff-ball", no one could have anticipated the lessons that would be learned from their adopted pet, Peter. As Ed and Peter share their words of wisdom the suggestions are powerful and could be applicable to all readers. Peter's experience of the world is simply lovely. He taught the family to "slow down". Time is fleeting. We should take a moment. Embrace each day. Each day is a new adventure. Consider seeing the world from someone else's point of view. Peter's sage advice to always make a good impression with those you meet is the first lesson in a master class in business. He led by example even during challenging situations. Peter never engaged in confrontations. He just walked away. World leaders could benefit from this strategy. Though many people struggle with past relationships, Peter offered insights that are more associated from a wise elder, "Humans need to shed the judgment from past experiences." Peter's experience of inter-animal and inter-species relationships encourage humans to "Get free of the past and approach the future without expectations." As a psychologist, I understand the value of his observations. Peter's words of wisdom are vital to the successful therapeutic process. We need to be, "More attentive to others' needs than our own." A powerful message for many readers will be Peter's gifted observation, "Be more intentional with your display of love". Ed has masterfully crafted a loving tribute to the impact of a "heart dog" can have on our lives. As you turn each page, you will find the lessons discussed throughout this book to be idyllic yet practical, heartfelt yet important to appreciate each day of your life.

—Dr. Harold Shinitzky, Psy.D. Licensed Psychologist. Author – A Champion's Mindset: 15 Mental Conditioning Steps to Becoming a Champion Athlete *(2018),* Take Control of Your Anxiety: A Drug-Free Approach to Living a Happy, Healthy Life *(2015),* Your Mind: An Owner's Manual for a Better Life *(2010). Past President of the Florida Psychological Association. 2022 Distinguished Service Award. Former faculty of the Johns Hopkins University, School of Medicine, Adolescent Clinic. Martin Luther King, Jr. National Award for Community Service*

PETER

*conversations with
a little white dog*

Edward J. Hickling

Illustrations by Edward J. Hickling
Book design by Jessika Hazelton

Printed in the United States of America
The Troy Book Makers • Troy, New York • thetroybookmakers.com

To order additional copies of this title,
contact your favorite local bookstore
or visit www.shoptbmbooks.com

ISBN: 978-1-61468-895-2

DEDICATION

To Linda, my family, and my mother
Phyllis. Without who I would have nothing.

To Leni and Gordon
I have such hope for you both.

And, to all who have loved and lost someone
and suffered that joy and pain.

EJH

Our family has had dogs for as far back as I can remember. As a child we had a small mixed breed beagle named Shultz who was full of energy and had a great howl. Then came Lumpy, a big mixed breed lab who largely liked to just lay around like a lump. There was no way to have a dog during my college and graduate school years. But once married and starting a family, we could now consider adding a dog to the mix. This was especially true after years of almost daily pleading by our sons before welcoming a wonderfully goofy Golden Retriever named Cobi.

While I loved all my dogs to pieces, what can happen if you are very, very lucky, is you will come across one of those truly wonderful dogs who fits into your lives almost like another child: a dog who is not only a beloved pet, but one who becomes a constant companion, a trusted confidant, and a significant part of the family. We're talking about a dog who is paws above the rest, and who seems to have been sent to you from a special place—perhaps even a heavenly or spiritual place—to share its life with you. Some people refer to such a dog as a "soul dog" or a "heart dog."

Such a dog possesses an extraordinary connection with us, as if they were destined to be by our sides—filling our lives with their unwavering loyalty, boundless love, and unique personalities. These are the dogs that imprint their pawprints on our souls and forever change us for the better.

Those who have had such a once-in-a-lifetime companion come to realize that, irrespective of life's challenges and joys, this one particular dog possessed an innate ability to show up at just the right moment: to lick tears and fill hearts with unwavering love.

This is the story of one such dog.

His name was Peter.

I don't remember much of anything except the date: January 14.

It was a rain-soaked Sunday morning, and I had taken it upon myself to climb out of our second-story window onto the roof to find the source of a leak. Seemed simple enough. I'd worked on roofs in my efforts to build a small cabin once upon a time not so long ago.

Keeping a firm footing was key.

I had the right positioning until I somehow didn't.

That's when my feet slid out from under me. I was suddenly sliding and grabbed hold of the gutter for dear life. Fortunately, I don't remember hitting the asphalt driveway, face first.

My wife, Linda, called 911.

All I remember is hearing a siren.

The bones in my face had shattered, along with multiple bones in my right arm, resulting in a LaForte III fracture. Translation? The bones in my face, including those around my eyes and in my nose and jaw, were shattered. So were multiple bones in my right arm.

Turns out, as I was later told, I was seriously lucky to be among the five percent of people who are reported to even survive such a fall—much less to come out without life-long physical and cognitive injuries.

During my hospital stay, I vaguely remember the surgeon informing my wife that they would need to wire my jaw shut prior to the operation. Additionally, she was informed about the potential risk: if I were to aspirate during the surgery, there was a chance they might not be able to establish an airway in time to save me.

Is this how our lives would end? At 52 years old and with two sons later? Well, actually, how my life would end?

Linda later told me the only thing that calmed her was a little white dog that a woman had kindly offered to provide emotional support. The dog apparently jumped into her lap, begging for affection, and sat with her the entire time she counted the ticks of the wall clock. Linda had decided right then and there, if the surgery went well—meaning if I made it out alive— she wanted to get a dog just like him.

How was it possible that just two weeks later, a little white dog just like him would bestow himself upon us?

Here's how these kinds of things happen: One day, a coworker of Linda's came to her for motherly advice. The issue was that she and her husband were growing worried about handling their household of three dogs with a new baby on the way—their first. They really loved their dogs, she told Linda, but there were now a bunch of unknowns. What if she and her husband were too exhausted to walk them on top of caring for a newborn? Worse, what if the dogs didn't take to the baby or what if the baby was allergic to dogs? Faced with these uncertainties and more, they made the tough decision to reduce the extra stress by finding new homes for the dogs.

Here's the clincher: Did Linda want one of their two Golden Retrievers? Wouldn't that be nice, considering we recently lost our own big goofy 85-pound lug of love, Cobi, to stomach cancer? None of us wanted a "replacement" Golden Retriever or even another dog for that matter.

Or did we?

Wait. What kind was their third dog? A 3 year old Bichon Frise? It sounded more like a fancy plate of curly lettuce than a breed of dog.

Ours was a family of hockey players—rough and tumble meat-and-potato boys, not French bistro types who wouldn't be caught dead walking a little white fluff ball. But Linda had already made up her mind. She felt the dog was "meant to be."

It seemed the dog had too.

Eager to make a winning first impression, the dog showed up for the meet and greet, fresh from the groomer who styled him in the traditional manner of presenting like a little white lion. This was apparently a "proper" look for a Bichon, to be all poofed out like he was competing for a blue ribbon in the Westminster Dog Show.

But the guise was really all in an effort to win us over to secure a new home.

Ours.

Our eldest, Matthew, took one look at the 17-pound toy of a dog, pronounced it a "pillow pet," and scoffed right out of the room.

I tried to be a bit more open-minded. I mean, that poor dog couldn't help having a bad hair day or that he now smelled like a skunk sprayed him with Jean Nate. He was also probably doubly freaked out, coming with his bag packed to stay at a stranger's house.

Only, he didn't let it show. Or at least, he hid it well. He was surprisingly calm—none of the stereotypical small dog behaviors such as yapping, hyperventilating, or peeing on the floor. This guy was super well-behaved, definitely not what we were used to in our house full of rowdy teenage boys and our lovable but not-so-bright Cobi, who would repeatedly clear the coffee table of all items with a single wag of his tail.

Michael, our youngest, strolled out from the kitchen. The dog earned only a sideways glance.

"No way!" he pronounced while continuing to annihilate a bag of potato chips. "That dog is not happening."

Matthew was now back on the scene to join forces with his brother.

"Come on, guys. I've seen bigger stuffed animals than him. I mean, if we're even going to get another dog, can't it be a real one?"

Linda and I tried to remain neutral, recognizing the dog was outnumbered four to one, as we debated whether to keep him. As for the dog, he simply just sat there, blinking his big brown eyes at the boys, then back at us, then back to the boys, then back to us. He was holding his space as if saying, "What have you got to lose? At least I'm cute!"

Only later did we learn that the dog was the swami of reading and adjusting to people's emotions. And right then, he knew his fate was teetering on teenagers. So he played it cool. Not too much and not too little. Just chill. His plan worked.

Linda and I had agreed to give it the weekend. Only then would we know whether it was a good fit for everyone involved—the little white fluff ball who called himself a dog obviously included.

First things first. Fluff Ball was intent on checking out the house, going from room to room, sniffing out his new surroundings. A couch here and a rug there. Oh, and what was behind that door? Something interesting? Maybe a snack? Or perhaps a second big comfortable chair that he would later claim as his personal napping kingdom?

"Isn't he cute?" Linda plied. "Just look at his little face, Ed!"

Translation?

"He stays."

Fluff Ball now seemed to understand that the key to completely sealing the deal was to approach each of us individually, almost as if seeking our blessing. Head down on his front legs. Brown eyes looking intently into ours. Tail wagging. Was he actually smiling? He clearly wanted to please us, despite feeling scared and probably sad and anxious at the same time.

He then employed an effective body language technique called "mirroring" in an effort to build further rapport. That meant if we sat down, he'd sit down. If we stood up, he'd stand up. If we moved around, he'd move around.

By now, he was clearly moving into our hearts.

And then into our bed when it came time to go to sleep.

While Cobi would jump up, sprawl out and take up every square inch, this guy waited for us to say it was ok before jumping up and snuggling in right next to us.

"Isn't he cute?" Linda coaxed. "I just love him!"

In the morning, Fluff Ball simply sat by the door, calmly waiting to be taken out.

I remember thinking how well he was adapting to being dropped into a completely foreign world: our home.

Correction: His home.

The boys were now in agreement: The dog stayed!

But there was still a slight problem. Fluff Ball's given name was Gizmo.

After hours of calling out name ideas like Bingo numbers, Michael excused himself to grab a bite to eat.

A few minutes later, he bound back into the living room, interrupting us with a one-word declaration.

"Peter."

The name just clicked.

And now Peter, the dog formerly referred to as Fluff Ball, but known as Gizmo, was part of the family.

And soon, the neighborhood.

It was on those three daily walks or by all calculations close to 16,000 excursions that my life experience changed.

Now, as I look back on our time together, it's almost as if Peter found purpose in teaching us to slow down and appreciate life through his perspective. As simple as it sounds, the lessons I learned from him are reflected in my daily life even now that he's gone as we "write" to each other to make more sense of the world.

PART ONE

Dear Peter,

Before long, you became the undisputed ruler of our house, although you never took advantage of your little superpower. Instead, you simply brought out the best in us. Linda, who you bonded with in a motherly, companion way by always being her sidekick, especially to get treats. Me, the meaningful psychologist who you taught to relate work experiences to our own experiences. Michael, who discovered how to be affectionate toward a small creature rather than the big, hairy, ball-catching beasts of dogs he grew up with. And Matthew, who would rush to greet you even before us when he came home on college breaks.

You taught us to see the world from your perspective, something that took time given that we are a family on the move. Sometimes you showed us patience, such as to give you time to stretch or yawn or stay hot on the trail of a fallen leaf before coming when called. In your mind, nothing was more important at that moment. To us, time used to feel like it was always rushing by, but thanks to you, we learned to slow down, at least some of the time.

We came to appreciate the beauty of taking a moment to fully observe—letting you dig in the snow before we shoveled it, or allowing you time to bask in the warm sun on a summer's day while listening to the birds' morning song, instead of brushing it off as mere background noise.

Your ability to communicate your willpower took a bit of time to adjust to but in the end, it's fair to say you trained us more than we did you.

Dear Ed,

First, let me express my gratitude for changing my name. Honestly, Gizmo was quite an odd choice for a dog like me! I mean, what were they thinking? I'm not some creature from the movie "Gremlins" who turns into a beast when it gets wet! And though I did my best to avoid rain and swimming at all costs, I must admit, I didn't hate going to that groomer. She was very pretty and really nice. But I do thank you for not letting anyone style my hair like that anymore.

Beyond that, I was more than willing to do my part, to be there for you, because, let's be honest, my dear humans, you could benefit from a little help understanding things from a dog's perspective. So please regard my words and thoughts as coming from my heart while I watch over you and strive to help you handle the emotions and memories you carry from our time together.

And now in your life without me.

Going back to the very beginning, I was indeed scared. And no, I doubt it would have taken a psychologist such as you to recognize it, but I do appreciate your insight and empathy given my situation. Meeting people for the first time is a nerve-wracking experience for anyone, but that day was especially intimidating for me because I knew I was leaving my family and attempting to become a part of yours.

This could have gone sideways quite quickly, so I made sure to be on my best behavior. No yapping, hyperventilating, or peeing on the floor as you said. (Not that I ever would, but just saying that little dogs get a bad rap sometimes.)

I suppose, even though I didn't have a say in it, our first life lesson together was to always make a good impression upon those you meet. That's why it's probably not always a bad thing to be a bit over-dressed than underdressed as people apparently form first impressions within seven seconds of meeting you or seeing you. So I guess that means you'll never get a second chance to make a good first impression.

You may be wearing the most out-of-place cloth-ing or sporting a bad haircut like mine or hiding behind an Instagram filter, but the real you can shine through if given a second chance. Sometimes, it means giving others the time they need to reveal their genuine selves. Remember, it isn't the cut of the cloth, but what's underneath that truly counts in making a relationship work. With time, when you're in the right place and able to be your authentic self, it becomes easier. You will be accepted and loved for who you are, not what you represent.

Dear Peter,

Taking you for a walk was almost always a pleasure. Each day that we ventured out the door and down the steps felt like the beginning of a new and exciting experience. It wasn't just about our special time together, but also about what you taught me. Through you, I learned to hit the pause button, even when you pulled on the leash to lead me on your treasure hunts. Each time you so excitedly went out the door, you approached each moment, each leaf and each blade of grass with such enthusiasm, as if every walk was the first– an adventure that held amazing treasures if we could only sniff them out.

I now try to live each day as a new opportunity for exploration, the same as you. As simple as that sounds, it's something us humans don't always do. We tend to bemoan running errands or making dinner or picking the kids up from school, whereas now I think of how lucky I am to have the ability to greet each day.

I also try to meet or say hello to new people in my daily life, the same as you did in meeting other dogs on our walks. To you, it didn't make a difference if the other dog outweighed you by 90 pounds, had a head as big as your whole body, or were pint-sized. Look out! It was game on! Peter was ready to play!

You'd begin by making eye contact and then once you got the other dog's attention, you'd bow your head down on your paws and stick your hind quarters straight up in the air before running in small, impossibly tight circles as if to say, "Catch me if you can!" These games of tag made us humans forget the day's monotonous responsibilities and enjoy the simple fun of watching our dogs play.

Or not.

Even when a potential friend let you know the answer was "no" through barking, growling, or pinning their ears back at you in a threatening way, you simply didn't engage in the confrontation. You just quietly moved on. And the walk would continue without any carry over or judgment.

I admire you for being able to do that. It's a lesson we can all learn in life: Not to engage in conflict or confrontation.

It was somewhat different with people. Your openness, friendliness and good cheer would win over even the surliest temperament. What a joy it was to see you bring a smile to a stranger's face. This is not to mention that the regulars on our routes often kept treats in their pockets, saved especially for you. Children would delight in your soft fur, bright eyes and willingness to be pulled into laps for endless petting.

My admiration grew even more while watching you handle a difficult situation while visiting my mother in the memory care unit at her nursing home. She loved your visits and treated you kindly, even when she might not have known who you or even any of her children were.

On one of those visits, however, a resident grabbed you by the throat without warning. One minute she was petting you and the next she was strangling you. Instead of nipping or growling, you demonstrated your serene, all-knowing wisdom by showing compassion for those less able to be the kind, considerate people you envisioned them to be. You simply looked at us with pleading eyes as if to say, "Please help me out here before I hurt this lady's feelings or she kills me!"

You displayed the same temperament with ducks. Yes, ducks. While most dogs can't resist chasing and barking at birds, you actually befriended them. Initially, Linda and I were tentative about leaving you behind when taking a quick business trip, even though you'd be staying with a kind, local veterinary assistant who babysat dogs. Well, dogs and ducks. Also cats. And other creatures.

We brought you over for an initial introduction and walked into a Dr. Doolittle menagerie. No crates. No isolation. Just love. Turns out, you even got to curl up and sleep in the family bed, a privilege not extended before, or since, to any other dog or animal. We hadn't asked, yet somehow, it just happened. This was not surprising given the impact you were able to have on all around you.

When we came to pick you up a few days later, you sprinted towards us, leading an ark-like procession that included a large white honking duck and three other dogs who were equally excited to greet us. It was a real spectacle, a parade if we ever saw one!

Dear Ed,

PS- Ducks can be pretty cool if you take the time to get past the honking.

But more to the point, if you poor humans could only shed the constraints imposed by your past experiences and expectations, what a difference it could make in your ability to grasp the significance of unconditional acceptance toward the world, and everyone and everything in it. Ducks included.

This is something you all should try to learn– to make every effort to improve yourselves with happy hearts and positive outlooks.

But how do we do that when we've had bad past experiences? In my case, I was separated from my litter, relocated to a new home with unfamiliar humans and two giant dogs, then cast out before even being given the opportunity to love and bond with a new baby. I loved that family and those dogs. And then, I was suddenly expected to cope with entering a strange new environment.

I decided it did not have to define who I was and how I wanted to live. The trick is to try to get free of the past and not fear the future. I mean, who knows what's coming? Possibly something good!

My approach was to accept hardships as the doorways to peace. I always tried not to have expectations of what you think will happen, because that can get in the way of what actually does happen. But I know, it's easier for most of us dogs. Humans come with more brain cells, but don't let it get you down. I believe you can learn this as well as any trick or command you tried to teach me.

Also, always keep in mind to greet and welcome everyone as they are in their unique place with joy, openness, and wholeheartedness. Even when faced with anger, choose to refrain from reacting and let it pass, all while acknowledging and appreciating others for who they are. This is a valuable lesson to hold onto. You're pretty good at it, but you can get even better. I have to believe that most people are trainable. You just have to have a very smart and awesome dog to help assist you in the process.

Dear Peter,

One of the most amusing things about you was your dedication to living up to the American Kennel Club's category for Bichons as companion dogs. You also fit nicely the inclusion as a therapy and emotional support dog. Everyone would agree, you took all these roles seriously by becoming a constant presence in our moment-by-moment lives. You were always right there. Close by. Really close by, in fact, like being attached to a leg or a hip or a head if we were lying down. You were 24/7/365. This marked a profound connection that evolved with each of us. You would establish eye contact, and then, if you could physically reach whoever it was, you'd eagerly join them. If you couldn't jump that high, you'd gaze up at them with those deep, dark, wise eyes as you lay in wait. You displayed extraordinary patience, even if your "target" left the room or made movements that might have unsettled a less emotionally attached dog who could have taken that as rejection. But you remained unfazed because you knew in your heart of hearts that eventually a hand would reach down to pull you up into a lap.

The tricky moments came when it wasn't clear who to attach yourself to. You had to figure out where to position yourself when we weren't all in the same room or when someone didn't seem to immediately need your company. Your solution? You'd find a spot where you could generally keep an eye on everyone and patiently wait for any cue to decide whether to move closer, hop into a lap, or settle down by someone's feet. This was often almost exactly the halfway point between you and the person. And even though I might want to believe you had favorites (like me), you treated everyone with equal amounts of love and affection. You found a way to demonstrate that everyone mattered to you, even the mailman, by not barking whenever he walked by.

Like a sentry on duty, you'd make your rounds to ensure you knew where everyone was located.

Kitchen. Check.

Yard. Check.

Bedroom. Check.

Only after completing your head count could you relax and settle into sleep. You were not just a companion dog; you were a dog who knew how to stay vigilant and ensure everyone was safe and accounted for.

The other thing is you'd never fully fall asleep until everyone was settled or asleep. Otherwise, you'd keep one eye open, watching for any signs of move- ment or activity. Once everyone was set and you'd made your rounds, you'd snuggle in … and snore! It wasn't a bothersome snore; in fact, it was peaceful. It only happened when you were truly at rest with- out any self-imposed duties. Hearing your soft, and sometimes not so soft sounds of peaceful sleep made everything feel just right - like all was well in the world. How I loved that sound.

You were a silent yet comforting presence especially during times of sickness, injury, or when someone felt low —a gentle shadow by our sides. Remarkably, during my recovery from the fall and months of follow up rehab, you hardly asked to go outside, remaining steadfastly beside me. And when you fell ill towards the end of your life, our roles reversed as we cared for each other.

I wrote this poem one night when I thought of you.

Joining

Tired, I lay down early,
Peter, at some point, begins his search,
Here, there, up, around
Until at last, after the hunt of familiar places,
discovers where I'm lying.
He circles, then collapses with resolve,
moving as close as he can to my posture of unrest
Head on my leg, back to my side in sweet repose

Me, in my half-awake state, notice his body
so still in its soulful peace,
the sound of his breath,
In and out, in and out,
calming my all too busy mind,
we join together

Inspired by Jane Kenyon, (1993). In and Out, In Constance, Graywolf Press. To view online, see: https://clodandpebble.wordpress.com/2012/07/ 11/in-and-out-by-jane-kenyon/

Dear Ed,

It feels good to be with those you love and to offer them comfort, peace and security. I guess that's why I always found it so puzzling when people avoid each other when they're in pain or need comforting. Dogs are lucky in that we don't have whatever it is that stops humans from showing their love and attention.

As dogs, we have a keen ability to sense when you're burdened by needs, doubts and pain which can cause you to act in ways you might not like or want. But even when we experience our own physical pain, we still strive to reach out to others selflessly. This ability can be learned, trust me on this. However, it's a path you must choose to follow. We dogs (and even some of you humans) do this for the greater good for those we love.

But sometimes people don't do it so reliably or so well. If you can embrace this lesson, to be more attentive to the needs of others and place your own needs second, it can make a big difference in your relationships. We can all show more care. None of us do all we can, even me, but that's where one starts.

Indeed, as a humble observer of human behavior, I must confess to occasional confusion regarding the peculiarities of your actions. However, it was an enlightening challenge. Allow me to impart some wisdom: be more intentional in displaying love. While you may never master this art as effortlessly as I did, making the attempt is worthwhile. Do you genuinely express your love to those dear to you or exhibit affection as frequently as you could? Do you say you love someone, or stay silent, believing "they know" you love them? It's a simple notion, yet I believe you could all benefit from a bit more practice in this area.

Dear Peter,

Why is it so hard for many of us to appreciate what we have? So often, it's because we fall into ruts, rarely noticing or embracing both the novel and the everyday experiences as being wonderful, full, and exciting. If we only approached each day like you did.

The challenge is we often slip into routines and embrace predictable ways of living and find ourselves either dwelling on the past or constantly looking ahead to the future. This is especially true when we feel stuck.

The challenge is to recognize that even in our seemingly mundane, routine lives, each moment is unique and will never happen exactly the same way again. By shifting our perspective and embracing each moment with appreciation and mindfulness, we can uncover the beauty and uniqueness that exists in our daily routines. It's like a baseball batter stepping up to the plate thousands of times, yet understanding that each at-bat is a one-of-a-kind opportunity to hit a home run. It's normal to get stuck from time to time, and even the best batters have slumps.

It's often said that dogs live in the moment. It certainly appeared true in your case, Peter. Throughout your life, you lived for each moment. It showed in your energy and your zest for playfulness, your cuddling, and your looking at us with those soulful, dark eyes, as if peering into our very souls. You were truly present.

If only some of that ability to connect with others and fully experience moments could rub off on our relationships, I think the world would be a happier place. Thank you for making me take a longer look at this in my own relationships and life.

I will always be reminded to adapt to new experiences when I think of how you handled traveling with us. Remember how the grass in Florida felt and looked so different under your paws? Unlike the soft, straight grass up north, it was all bunchy and slightly rough. Watching you trying to make sense of these new sensations was like watching a man walk on the moon. Yet once again, you embraced something completely new by taking tentative step after tentative step almost like tip toeing. Soon enough, you began running in happy circles.

The other experience that stands out is when we moved to that condo with elevators. You embraced the same sense of novelty when it came time to enter a small room, feel it move upward, and then arrive in a completely different place. Surprisingly, it didn't seem to faze you. Nor did walking across a bridge more than 100 feet above the ground while we were on a sight-seeing excursion. I was somewhat nauseous, but you simply kept going. Life was to be embraced, wherever you were or whatever you were doing.

Still, the one thing you never wavered on was swimming or really even getting wet for that matter. It's rather surprising given the historical role of Bichons as sea dogs that aided Spanish sailors during their voyages.

But hey, to each his own.

You definitely had, shall we say, distinct preferences, and water-related activities simply weren't high on your list. This included baths and a definite lack of enthusiasm for swimming, even in the Atlantic Ocean, though you didn't mind walking on the beach and running and playing at the water's edge with newfound friends. Rainy days weren't exactly your favorite either. Hence, the little yellow raincoat we suited you up in whenever the weather wasn't cooperating.

In the spirit of Buddhist philosophy, it was as if you carried your presence and joy with you wherever you ventured by truly living in the present moment - come hell or high water.

Dear Ed,

I still can't believe I did it! I think that my determination to face getting wet, crossing that dizzyingly-high bridge, riding in that suffocating contraption you call an elevator, and even subjecting my paws to that brittle grass was my way of trying to inspire you to embrace life in a similar manner. Well, except for climbing on roofs and ladders; we all remember how that turned out.

If it weren't for you, I never would have even seen, much less played in the ocean. It took bravery because we all know I don't like water, except when it's in my dog bowl.

It seems that most humans often get caught up in striving for safety, perceiving danger everywhere, and consequently filling your minds with worry and fear. Maybe stop that so that new experiences aren't seen through the lens of potential pain. I guess that's why you don't walk barefoot in the grass, instead choosing to wear shoes in case you step on a rock? I say, go bare-pawed all the way!

Dear Peter,

I just found one of your toys under the couch. It made me so sad that I cried. God I miss you. This particular toy was not for any special reason. Actually none of them really were. You just loved toys so much that they weren't just given to you on holidays, birthdays or because you had done some wonderful new thing that we rewarded. You got new toys all the time.

Some dogs are particularly fond of grab-and-pull toys like knotted ropes that they can latch onto with their mouths for a good game of tug of war. Others love to chase. You throw a ball, and they're off to the races!

But you? Out of all of your toys, squeaky ones were always the favorites. It was a simple case of cause and effect: when you chewed on the plastic, air was forced out through the squeaker which made the noise. The best part is once squeezed, the shape of the toy returned and you got to do it all over again. Some dogs go completely nutso in swinging the toy back and forth as if it's a real critter. They love making the noise, each and every time.

You were no exception!

It was a never-ending cycle of chomp, squeak, repeat. We loved watching you go all action-hero, swinging them around like you were in an epic battle to save the queen, albeit against a stuffed animal.

But your mission was not to make it squeak. That was just a bonus. The goal was to get that squeaker out of the toy as fast as you could to hunt it, shake it, chew it, paw at it, lift it into the air, and chew some more until that glorious moment when the squeaker finally popped out from its fluffy prison. It was like you won the doggy lottery: Peter the champion squeaker liberator!

The only other toy that came close to the squeakers were the ones we stuffed with treats. Little did you know that the interactive contraption was designed to challenge a dogs' problem-solving skills. In this case, yours. It was so amusing to watch you master the art of finding every single treat every single time though you didn't always eat every single one of them. I wonder why? I mean who can leave one lone cookie on the plate?

Dear Ed,

Achieving things in life takes a lot of effort, and you certainly gave me some great reasons to work toward goals. Whether it was me learning to adapt with just one eye later on in life or figuring out how to silence that annoying squeak in all those stuffed animals, you kept me busy.

So yes, I did like the challenge of those so-called interactive toys. (I knew what you were doing, by the way, but I went along with it.) To me, it was just fun. But man, some of the time, it took work, especially on the chew resistant ones. Still, it was totally worth it! To me, there's something truly satisfying about doing the same thing over and over again until you reach your goal. It gave me a real "I can do this" attitude. What did that guy Albert Einstein say? "I have tried 99 times and have failed, but on the 100th time came success."

It's kind of like the days after your accident when I watched you start with two pound weights, then gradually increase them to five, then ten, and finally, an impressive twenty pounds. That's what I'm talking about. Pushing through to reach your goals.

So yes, you can teach an old dog new tricks! Even you, as I see you getting older now too. Keep the faith, my friend. You only get so many opportunities in life.

Now, regarding how I knew when to stop even if some treats remained, well, that's a life skill, my friend – the mastery of not overindulging. Good luck, and keep trying!

Dear Peter,

You were always such a happy, easy going little guy, allowing us to bring you anywhere, anytime without incident. We affectionately dubbed you our "pack and play" dog for this very reason. Regardless of the location or circumstances, you greeted every situation with

enthusiasm, never displaying any signs of aggression –
no bites, growls, or barks, even when provoked. I had
never even heard you bark for that matter. Not once…
Not until… the Florida road trip.

That's when you surprised us.

As you know, dogs can also experience grief and
emotional distress when someone they're deeply
bonded with, like their human, passes or moves away.
Or in your case, gives you away to a new family. There
are numerous stories of dogs mourning the loss of their
owners by sitting by their graves or by waiting at the
door, hoping for their return. These behaviors demonstrate that dogs can feel absences and can grapple with
the emotional void left behind. It's a testament to the
strong bonds and emotional connections that dogs
form with the people in their lives.

I'm certain that's what triggered your reaction to
that dreadful, OMG first night on the road at the "dog
hotel." You must have thought we died or at least left
you alone to die. I still feel guilty to this day and I'm
so sorry for not recognizing our mistake. But in our
defense, here's the story.

Linda and I thought you would be totally fine with
us ducking out of the hotel room to grab a fast bite to eat.
We'd only be gone about 45 minutes but obviously made
sure to get you all settled in with your favorite blanket,
toys, and extra food and water after a "just in case" walk.

When we got back to the hotel, we were literally
shocked that the manager said our dog had been wail-

ing and barking his head off the entire time we were gone. There was no way! He insisted "yes way" and to prove it, showed us numerous complaints from guests for our room, #117.

I remember saying, "There must be a mistake. Our dog NEVER barks."

In fact, during check-in, we proudly told the clerk as he petted you how your breed doesn't shed, is hypoallergenic, and notably, in your case, never barked. (It's true. We never heard you bark, though once in a great while you'd make a little peculiar throaty noise.)

What all of this meant was he must have had the wrong dog!

Only, the closer we got to the room, the more pronounced the barking became. Could that really be coming from Peter? Where was he? Did another dog get in our room? Was Peter possessed? We opened the door to find you frantically running around the room, trembling with wide fear-filled eyes. It made us cry to see our little guy in such a state of panic as we rushed to hug and comfort you.

Peter, we are so sorry! We never thought us leaving would affect you like that. Lesson learned. It was a strange place with strange smells and we left you there alone. We would never do that again!

The good thing about you is that soon, everything was ok in your world again.

Dear Ed,

I guess I taught you that human psychology can be applied to dogs. I understand your thinking that all the love you gave me would erase any deep-seated abandonment issues that may have been lurking in my little soul. I truly do understand as you share our thought process, but never take for granted how much others may need you, especially in what they might see as new and maybe scary circumstances like a strange home or hotel room.

So now you see that dogs aren't so different from people after all.

Granted, most of us have been surprised to see someone we know act scared or out of character. Please don't assume that you really know what anyone else's experience will be even if the circumstances seem neutral and non-threatening. Yes, we all make assumptions. And yes, I forgive you. Don't beat yourself up too badly. It was an honest mistake made better by the extra toys and treats you bestowed upon me for the rest of the trip. And yes, I could bark, but only when I had something to say. I definitely had something to say that night! But you listened, and that is also everything.

Dear Peter,

I wanted to share another poem with you.

Otherwise

I got out of bed
on two strong legs.
It might have been
otherwise. I ate
cereal, sweet
milk, ripe, flawless
peach. It might
have been otherwise.
I took the dog uphill
to the birch wood.
All morning I did
the work I love.

At noon I lay down
with my mate. It might
have been otherwise.
We ate dinner together
at a table with silver
candlesticks. It might
have been otherwise.
I slept in a bed
in a room with paintings
on the walls, and
planned another day
just like this day.
But one day, I know,
it will be otherwise.

I hope you feel the significance of these words. They remind us that nothing stays the same and that change is inevitable, even if we don't wish for it to be so. Dogs, and you in particular, had always been viewed as stoic. If life dealt you a blow, you sized it up, accepted it, and moved on. Not like us humans who tend to carry a lot of things as changes occur both in us and around us.

As for your eye, I don't know exactly when it started, but there were times when you would simply sit and stare off into space. We joked that you might be contemplating the universe or meditating. The thing was, your overall demeanor didn't change so we weren't worried- just confused. You still had blasts of puppy-like energy as you carried on with your life eating, playing, and walking with us. It was puzzling, but not alarming as you were getting older and perhaps just taking it easier.

What did we really know?

Apparently, not enough according to Google when we had asked, "Why does my dog stare off into space?" The list of possibilities went on. Heightened hearing and smell? Boredom? A bug on the wall? Ohh! Wait. Could it be eyesight related? Maybe you couldn't see as well as you used to. After all, you were now 11 years old, equivalent to being in your 70's in dog years. Linda and I wore glasses too. The search engine said - get this - that among a few other breeds, Bichon's can be predisposed to vision problems.

We made an immediate appointment with the vet. Well, several vets, until we found the right one. Indeed, you tested for cataracts but worse, one of the lenses in your eye had become detached. This, we were told, was also common.

But the worst part is the vet said it was an incredibly painful condition. The guilt we experienced was overwhelming because we had no way of knowing. You never squinted, closed your eyelid, or displayed any signs that you were in pain. You were as stoic as stoic could be.

Now, it was you who needed surgery.

The eye specialist explained that there was no guarantee the lens could be reattached. If not, we would have to confront the decision to either remove the eye or proceed with a second surgery to remove it if necessary. The procedure was called an enucleation.

At home, we read up on every aspect of the condition. The dog ophthalmologist mentioned the primary side effect would be hair growing over your eye socket which would make it look like you were winking. It sounded somewhat endearing, but the post-op photos we saw online were far from cute. It didn't look like any wink we'd ever seen in dogs or in people.

There had to be another way.

But the online groups and all of our dog-loving friends who we bombarded with questions about their own experiences and knowledge shared stories of success. Most importantly, and overwhelmingly, we needed to get you out of pain. So ultimately, we chose the surgery.

The recovery was hard. You were not happy that first day, but allowed me to hold you in my lap while Linda drove us home. I had never seen you tremble, or look so small and scared, even in the hotel room on the way to Florida. As I cradled you, wrapped in your favorite blanket, I carried you as gently as I could into our home. You seemed so fragile at that moment, almost like a baby.

We never left your side.

By the second week, your miraculous energy was almost back to normal, just as the veterinarian had said. The hardest part would be you adjusting to life with only one good eye.

In the beginning, we'd get ahead of you to clear a safe path free of hazards and objects you could potentially, and inevitably, run into such as an open kitchen cabinet or a pair of sneakers by the front of the door. Do you remember when you fell off the last step of the porch? The look on your face was actually funny, like "huh, what just happened?" as you got up and shook yourself off with grace and good humor.

I admired you for holding your own, something I was less capable of doing after my own surgery, and certainly not with your grace.

Dear Ed,

E new? E nuc lee? E what? I'm just a little dog. And that was such a big word to try to pronounce.

All I can say is I'm truly grateful you didn't allow that first vet to test my vision as he suggested by putting me in a dark room full of obstacles like tires and chairs to see if I ran into anything. Pardon the pun, but that guy seemed to be living in the dark ages of medicine! I mean who wouldn't run into things in the dark?! Did he really go to vet school?

I liked and trusted the second vet much better. She knew exactly what she was doing which helped me feel way less vulnerable and scared. Thank you for staying by my side until I went to sleep. And for being there the second I woke up. That helped a lot after having your eye removed to have your humans right there. You and Linda were both so kind and caring. I really appreciated it. But who knew the neighbors would bring me treats and presents? That was soooo nice of them. Everyone was so supportive in helping me heal and adapt. Well, except for that porch step.

Do note that while I was indeed an awesome patient, it's in a dog's genetic make-up to adapt to different physical demands and to recover quickly from injuries. It's an eat or be eaten means of survival out there in the wild. Yes, that translates even to your suburban living room where that zebra striped pillow could have come after me at any point.

But seriously, you were so good to me throughout my life. I've witnessed dogs being mistreated by their owners, and as a result, they live in constant fear. Even when placed in loving homes, they may remain cautious and unable to let people get too close for fear of getting hurt again. However, their remarkable resilience allows them to rise above their past over time and to find love and happiness once again. These stories of triumph over adversity serve as a powerful reminder of our indomitable spirit. This is probably why we are called man's best friend.

Know that you were my best friend, too.

I've heard you counsel people who have lost a loved one or who have been deeply hurt by someone or something. I wonder why some humans can learn to move forward in life by reconciling their emotional pain while others find it very difficult. To a dog, it seems like some people can remain trapped in the past, struggling with what once was, and consequently carry that pain with them, even as life and time moves on.

Drawing from my own experiences from weathering emotional trauma and overcoming physical injuries, my lesson would be to accept what you cannot change, change what is possible, and do everything you can to continue being a part of the life you have. It can be a challenging path to follow, but it is achievable in the right setting with the right approach and lots of support.

Maybe you're companion people?

Dear Peter,

Do you remember when Michael and his wife Abbie said they wanted a dog "just like Peter?"

What a compliment! They came close, too! The dog they fell in love with during an online search was called a Bich-poo; half Bichon Frise and half Poodle. The breed was also a bit smaller, about 12 pounds. Otherwise, it looked like a total mini-you!

Wisely, they sought my sister Judy's advice. She and her husband, John, are super active in agility training and over the years have learned a lot about dogs. These are two real and true outdoors people, and now that they're retired, they have even more time to dedicate to their dogs. Their extensive network within the dog community and experience with various breeds and breeders and all things related to dogs have been instrumental in offering assistance and guidance to anyone and everyone, including us.

Everything she said was not what Mike and Abbie wanted to hear. First, they were told not to buy a dog unless they knew a lot about the breeder and the breeder's history and track record. Good breeders, she said, love their dogs, and will always take the dog back for any reason if it doesn't work out.

They knew nothing about the breeder.

This was not off to a good start.

Second question. Where was the dog breeder located?

"Don't tell me Missouri," she said point blank.

Answer?

"Missouri."

Sorry Missouri, it's a reputation thing. No offense. I'm sure there are many really good breeders in Missouri, but right or wrong, the Midwest has a reputation for being home to a fair number of puppy mills, where the quality of the puppies can be mixed, and you can't be sure without more information. You may well get a dog with a lot of up and coming health problems, and other things that a reputable breeder looks out for, and is aware of in their breeding of dogs.

Third, she said, if you do choose an out-of-state breeder who you don't know anything about, please don't pick a breed like a Bich-poo.

OMG!

She said they don't have the stamp of approval from the American Kennel Club because if the mixed breed dog (Bichon and miniature or toy Poodle) were to have offspring, it is uncertain as to what the health implications could be. There might be issues like dislocated kneecaps better known as luxating patellas for one. What this meant is the breeder may not have had the health and well-being of the dog in mind, but instead could just be trying to make a cute puppy. Now, I don't know how much of that is true or not, all I can say is what I was told and how I remember it. Hours were spent in discussion.

So, you can imagine, with all this learned advice from someone you love and trust, it would at least put some doubt into a reasonable person's head. But not Michael and Abbie's. If anything, it made their resolve to get the dog even stronger. They were already head over heels in love with her and there was no turning back now.

The next thing we knew, the dog was being flown into our local airport. And she was, of course, absolutely adorable.

They decided to name her none other than Judy.

My sister took it in good humor, wishing them the best. The best in fact happened, as "Judy" turned out to be and is a great dog.

What's more, Peter, you couldn't have been happier! A new playmate had arrived right in your own living room! Only she was a 5-pound squirt with ahem… abundant energy… who proved herself capable of wiggling and running even faster than you. She looked so much like a mini-me version of you it was like seeing double. You immediately welcomed her and tolerated all of her puppy antics which were undeniably cute, but could also be a bit challenging to handle at times.

You taught her how to play chase and engaged her in your favorite game of running in circles. Judy was quick, but she never quite embraced playtime as fervently or for as long as you did. But, true to your welcoming, tolerant personality, the two of you became fast friends even when she tugged on your tail or jumped onto your back.

I believe this friendship, and maybe even a type of "dog mentoring," or perhaps the welcoming of a "young un" into the pack, brought more vitality to your life. She certainly made it harder for you to take naps, although she would always eventually join you.

Dear Ed,

Having friends is a wonderful thing, even when they seemingly drop out of the sky from an airplane and decide to take over your spot on the couch. It's all good. You just have to be patient when they occasionally get on your nerves by sitting on your head or making off with your squeaky toys.

I had never come across a Bichpoo before, especially not one that I was supposed to love and even somewhat tolerate, but I did. I genuinely loved Judy. My job or role, as I saw it, was to be her teacher. I felt the need to share in lessons and experiences as a way of guiding her and instructing her. It is something really special when a bond like ours forms. Older dogs definitely have valuable lessons to share with younger ones, if you can cultivate that trust. And oh yes, that tolerance.

I saw you do that, too, with your patients and with the young ones who came into your life - kids, daughters-in-law, and your grandchild. It's a good thing and natural thing to mentor others, as long as we allow them the space to grow independently.

As we all know, things inevitably come to an end when nature decides to take its course. Dogs can sense these things and Judy knew I was beginning to become unwell even before my health began to really deteriorate. I knew it too. I could feel my body changing but I felt certain when she stopped trying to get me to play as much and started giving me the toys rather than making off with them. She also began to let me eat first and gave me back my spot on the couch and would then snuggle up next to me. I knew the day was coming, but it was ok. I had lived a wonderful life and was lucky enough to actually get a baby to love. Puppy or human, it made no difference. But I got both Judy and your grandson, Gordon.

I had so much love to give and I am so thankful for the opportunity to bestow it upon them. My life had now come full circle. I was able to live out my purpose and take pride in my achievement of passing the proverbial bone.

It made me sad to see you so sad, but what is that expression or movie called? All dogs go to heaven?

Edward J. Hickling

Dear Peter,

We humans have a saying that "getting old is not for the weak." As it happens, we often regale each other with stories about doctor visits, test results and aches and pains. One older client told me he and his friends talk about their ailments and bodily functions so much because they're continuously astounded at the newness of being old.

There were unmistakable indications of you slowing down as you aged alongside us over the years – more frequent naps, the emergence of cataracts followed by losing your eye. It wasn't long before it seemed like your hearing might be fading as well. Growing old is undeniably challenging, especially for dogs whose entire lives are compressed into seven human years for each year of canine existence.

But then you would surprise us with sudden bursts of energy. This happened especially when your little buddy Judy came around, but also during our playful game of slapping my thighs like a drummer to see if you were in the mood for some doggy playtime. When you were up for it, you'd dash and dart with such pure joy and boundless enthusiasm that even Judy would have had a hard time keeping up with you.

Over time, those energetic bursts became less frequent, replaced by more moments of panting and lying down afterwards. Yet, when we held you on our laps during car rides, snuggled next to you on the couch, and listened to your gentle snores that eased us into sleep at night, it felt like those moments would last forever. Those times, watching you bask in the sun, a joy you had held onto from puppyhood through your older years, were moments of serenity and tranquility. We found solace in sharing those simple pleasures, doing nothing but watching the grass grow together.

Dear Ed,

Us dogs can't luxuriate in the decades of life most people have. Perhaps that's why we are so happy to greet each day whereas humans often seem to dread their days upon days. And then they rush around doing this and that. For what? They are often missing the moments by not pausing to even breathe or stop and smell the bushes.

In observing the people who came into my life, it seemed many found it hard to break free of their roles or the assigned roles they laid upon their own tables. Many were sad or at least not happy. I'm lucky as a dog, my role is perhaps less complicated by busy thoughts. It probably helped that we don't have opposable thumbs to make and use tools (just no more ladders!) and grow bigger brains. We should all at times act silly, to join in with grandkids, and dance (or run around if you're a dog). Life will pass in a moment. What remains is the memory of stepping inside of who we are, and outside of ourselves when we feel trapped in a role that doesn't make us happy. Even us dogs, unique as we are, seek acceptance from those around us. But as we age, it becomes important to tap into our energy now and then to find the happiness in our lives. Afterward, it's equally important to rest among those who care for us deeply. It's a lesson I hope to share with you for all your days, however long or short they may be.

Dear Peter,

Love is like a coin. On one side, you have all the good stuff like joy, fun, and closeness that make it so special. But, as poets often say, all love is doomed. It's just a matter of time until one or the other will die; and then you are left with the pain, the loss, the sorrow- the other side of the coin.

Watching you deteriorate forced me to acknowledge the darker side of the coin. This pain, I've realized, defines the depth of the relationship and serves as a measure of the emotions and attachment that existed.

This is why it's essential never to dictate to a grieving parent how quickly they should recover from the loss of a child, or to a grieving spouse coping with the loss of a life partner. My role at work is to help people face and hopefully find a way to reconcile the grief that comes with losing someone or something that defined their lives. Loss is an inevitable part of life, yet we often make great efforts to avoid our new realities by living in the past or by giving up hope and dreams. Or we make great efforts to try to forget, to bury our feelings, but we never truly heal.

Similarly, this has been true for me in coping with the losses I've encountered in my own life – the passing of parents, a brother, friends, and patients. Yet, somehow, it was your death that reaffirmed the profound acknowledgement of how much love can hurt. It granted me greater permission to embrace such strong emotions unlike other losses that carried more intricate and multifaceted processing. Strange how once again a special dog can allow feelings that are so present, yet not always available as we grieve our human loved ones? I think of it as one more gift that such a special attachment and bond can exist.

As we all understand without needing any lectures, impermanence is a fact of life. Instead of anticipating the pain to completely vanish, if we perceive it as a reflection of the love experienced in the relationship, it becomes a poignant reminder of the beautiful moments. Perhaps, the intensity of pain signifies the depth of the love that existed. Naturally, there might be regrets about how things could have been different.

The relationship with a dog is clean and simple. There's an unbridled beauty in that purity of connection that makes the grief that much harder to escape.

Edward J. Hickling

Feelings of guilt often arise when we scrutinize our actions in hindsight, dwelling on the "what if's." This can serve as a form of self-punishment or as a way to avoid accepting the reality of the situation. We then tend to question if our emotions adequately match the depth of the relationship and the weight of grief we bear.

The experience of suffering such profound emotional pain reaffirms just how important you were to me. I actually feel a sense of human gratitude for our ability to feel deeply, knowing that we can grow from our experiences. That understanding enables us to cherish those who are still present in our lives, ensuring that we never forget their value and the loving connections we share.

When you hear people say, "It was only a dog," you know they will never understand.

Dear Ed,

I miss my human. I loved our home and my pack. The reminder of the losses in life also helped me value how much people, and other dogs, really make a difference in our lives, and that to do so means there has to be room for pain. But I know as a dog, part of my job is to show you in my shortened life how the cycle goes forward, and how we embrace both sides of the coin, as you say.

I hope you are able to, in part, see it as a good pain, that awful feeling that only comes when there is love. You people can be complicated in your efforts to sort out your feelings. I hope that as the dog in your life, as you say "that special dog," I can show you a way to better understand the feelings that are so hard to put into words, yet impact us so strongly.

Dear Peter,

You encountered numerous opportunities to express anger or hurt, especially with other dogs or certain people. During our walks, some dogs would

Edward J. Hickling

challenge you with growls and threats, attempting to provoke a reaction, yet you just continued on. It amazed me how you maintained your composure. You wouldn't look away, yet you didn't retaliate. It was as if you had a distance between their provocation and your own principals. This also applied to squirrels and cats—while other dogs would chase them, you simply acknowledged their presence and continued on.

Most often, when someone or something provoked you, your response was one of patience or puzzlement, of showing indifference rather than of escalating the situation. Even if some didn't seek your friendship, you would simply move on and seek new connections. You consistently avoided displaying anger, even in instances when children were overly rough while playing with you—an admirable trait.

When confronted, you seemed surprised but never lost sight of who you were and how you chose to respond. You assessed the situation, acknowledged those present, and reacted in ways that served your purpose. Your ability to avoid anger was remarkable in a world where most succumb to it.

There might have been times where anger could have been justified, yet you never exhibited it. It didn't come across as weakness or avoidance; rather, you did things your way—a manner I still struggle to emulate at times. It wasn't about running away or seeking protection; it was your unique approach. Gandhi would have been proud. I know I was.

Dear Ed,

Namaste. (I knew that phrase would come in handy at some point in time!) Why would I need to give in to anger? There are certainly other alternatives. I suppose I happened to be wired for handling it better than others. If there's a lesson for me to impart from all of this, and it seems there is, it's that one must be absolutely certain that their response is the one they'd want to be remembered for.

In life, for most of us, and in most situations we encounter, it just isn't worth stooping to someone else's level. When we do, we tend not to like our response and wish we could have done something different, something kinder or smarter. There is almost always a more peaceful path to follow. And remember, I'm just a little fluff ball. The world is teeming with much larger creatures that could potentially harm me at any given moment. However, if I had let that fear dictate my life from the start, it wouldn't have allowed me to lead the life I enjoyed, doing things my way, the peaceful way. So, if a little white dog like me can discover that path, perhaps there's hope for the rest of you too?

Edward J. Hickling

PART TWO

Dear Ed,

I know you could have died in the hospital after your accident. And I'm sorry I wasn't there to be by your side, but I didn't know you yet. From all the bits and pieces I overheard in various conversations, this clearly wasn't an easy time for you or your family. Although it certainly got better once I got there, if I say so myself. I liked keeping you company and being by your side.

It always struck me that you didn't even call out the staff for accidentally dropping you on the floor when moving you from your bed or by failing to provide pain medication for 12 hours after surgery due to that malfunctioning machine. You didn't even get upset when the ambulance driver in-training drove right by the emergency department entrance. You said you wanted the last impression that you would leave on someone to be one of dignity and respect- kindness over anger and restraint over agony as your final legacy.

In my own experiences as a patient in animal hospitals, I realize that things weren't always ideal, but once more, I attempted to embrace the circumstances, accept my reality, and aspire to leave a lasting impression just like you did. It's true, dogs might exhibit stoicism, yet trust me, we can also feel fear and apprehension in response to our surroundings.

I guess we're not dissimilar after all.

Dear Peter,

Allowing new people into your life can indeed be challenging. More often than not, it's the friends we made during our school years, from grade school to high school, and later in college and the workplace, who remain our steadfast companions. These are the friends we rely on in times of joy and trouble. When we establish a strong and enduring bond early on, it enables us to grow together, even when there may have been years of separation as we start families and become absorbed in our work.

Although we might develop many acquaintances, deep and enduring friendships seem to occur less frequently or without a significant amount of shared history. This shared history could emerge from scenarios such as parents raising children together simultaneously or from intensely demanding work situations, as commonly experienced in fields like medicine.

We had the incredibly good fortune of having both old and new friends, but also to have a grandson join our family. And like many grandparents, we immediately bonded and saw him as a precious, vulnerable, unique, and intimate part of our world.

It was truly heartwarming to witness the deep friendship you formed with him which is exactly what I'm talking about. You sought him out the moment he arrived in our home and forged an instant connection. It was remarkable how from the very day Gordon entered our lives as a newborn, you never left his crib or his side as he achieved milestones like sitting up, crawling, and eventually walking. You were constantly positioning yourself between this precious little baby and the world, always ready to protect him from any potential harm.

As our grandson transitioned from a baby to a toddler and then a young boy, the dynamics of play between the two of you evolved. Despite his developing motor skills sometimes resulting in less-than-gentle petting or hugs, you understood how to behave, aiding Gordon's growth and learning in this unique relationship. Over time, you developed a deep friendship. You played together, shared sleeping spaces, and often cuddled on the couch. Although it might still be considered a companion role, you took it upon yourself to become Gordon's watchdog, always ensuring his safety and well-being.

Dear Ed,

Wow, that brings back memories. Yes, Gordon was great. I do love babies, and little people closer to my own size. He also liked to play a lot more than bigger people often did. Yes, new arrivals are great and one should celebrate the rarity of it happening.

Not everyone gets a litter that adds to your pack. When it happens, it's a beautiful thing, especially for me since I lost out on loving my first family's baby.

You benefit from having the willingness to change your own behavior to fit the needs of that new person over yourself. It's not just them getting the benefit of you giving to them. It's a two-way street. This of course is true in any relationship, including the ones we had over time. We can sometimes make it hard to let new people or even new dogs into our lives. The willingness to treat someone who is more vulnerable, someone in need of your protection can be learned, and it is almost always possible to do so with grace and kindness.

But this is not always the case. I've talked to other dogs who didn't feel secure when a new baby came into the home. They would act mean, or pull away as if the baby was somehow a threat. They were afraid, and often correctly so, that there would be less time for them in the family. If so, in any situation in life, you just find your spot. New litters are born. Each of us have a place, not a smaller place, but one that is a change and needs to be seen as such a wonderful opportunity.

For me it was even more special. Remember, I lost my brothers and family before I joined this one. They were great dogs and people, but new ones can be found and when you earn your spot, love unfolds.

I miss Gordon.

Edward J. Hickling

Dear Peter,

I often say it's important to be lucky in life. While many things can impact the path of our lives, both good and bad, luck certainly has a part (or fate if you are so inclined). I don't know why you came into our lives. I don't know the answers as to why things happen the way that they do or did. But I do know you came to us in a way that seems almost magical. We were so lucky.

I think of you and our time together as a gift in terms of the impact you had on all of our lives. Perhaps, if we look, many things are there as gifts. Conversations with friends, glorious sunsets, paintings, music, and the ability to appreciate our lives.

Relationships are almost always the thing that people say is most important as they reflect on their lives. It's like the saying that no one ever wishes they worked more hours, but almost to a person, we all wish that we had more time with family, spouses, kids, grandkids, friends, and in this case, you Peter.

Dear Ed,

I believe you possess a pretty good understanding of both the human and canine experience, and these insights have contributed to shaping the person you are today. (See, you're catching on!) The beauty of life surrounds us in every moment. We never anticipated developing the remarkable bond that emerged from our time together. I acknowledge that, at times, we recognized the significance of these moments as they unfolded. Our hearts were frequently filled with wonder and joy. However, I'm also certain that we (perhaps more on your part than mine, although even dogs have their imperfections) didn't fully grasp and cherish this gift as often as we could have. This, too, is part of the ongoing realization that continues to unfold through memories, even to this day. The fact that both of us are reminiscing about our shared experiences and attempting to make sense of them is a gift in itself, wouldn't you agree? I certainly do. Memories are an integral part of our time together, a gift that persists as you smile or reflect on the past, appreciating the moments we've shared.

Dear Peter,

Looking back, it's funny that my son Michael grappled for so long over whether to shave or not to shave his beard for his wedding. The decision of how he would remember the day in his mind and through photographs was heavily-weighed. By him and by extension, me.

At the time, it seemed fairly insignificant and re-minded me of when we would all grow impatient and slightly annoyed when you would scratch and scratch and scratch and dig and dig and dig at your blanket until you got it just right before settling in. Sometimes we even yelled "Stop!" Then you'd just look at us like, "What is your problem, people? I'm just trying to get comfortable here."

Did all the fussing really make a difference in the quality of your sleep the same as whether Michael's back and forth, and forth and back about the facial hair would affect his wedding day?

But the question remained. Would he keep a full beard? Or go clean shaven? Or just keep the mustache? At least he had a choice, unlike you who emerged from the groomer looking like an explosion of cotton candy-a four legged pom pom.

I went from scolding you for digging and now feel-ing guilty about it, to learning to keep my mouth shut.

In the end, as the story goes, Michael shaved the beard and kept the mustache, the same as I had on my own wedding day 46 years ago and counting. He felt it would give him good luck.

Now that you're gone, I would give anything to watch you go through the annoying process of nesting just one more time. And I will always remember that when I look at Michael's wedding photos.

Dear Ed,

I may have dug a bit more just to get a rise out of you, to show you that I was the pint-sized boss of my own blanket, thank you very much. The thing is, if you must know, it's important to get your blanket just right to sleep really, really well. I needed to go through that circling behavior to get comfortable, but also to test your patience. It's really those little things that you reflect back upon as the big lessons in life, even if it's not clear to you at the time.

Later, when the blanket is folded and put away or when the photos have faded, we recognize these moments are gone- the moments are sometimes the very things that we may miss most of all.

Dear Peter,

I will always remember our last times together.

At the end of February, the weather broke and there was finally a nice day in upstate New York. There was still a chill in the air, but it was warm enough to go outside. The snow had melted a bit and there were places to smell and not have your paws get cold and wet. There was even grass exposed under trees and near driveways where the plows had been. We decided to take you for a walk. You had been more sick over the past few days, but could rise up from time to time and this seemed like something worth doing.

We went to see the neighborhood, knowing it might be the last time, and to offer you the chance to smell the things that had been such a big part of your life. You moved so slowly. Each step seemed etched in time, and needed to be taken in as fully and as memorably as we could. Linda and I moved slowly too as we walked along with you. Each pause and smell was precious. You seemed at times to be in pain, but you kept on going. You must have known it was important to spend this time together, to say goodbye to this part of our lives.

We ran into a neighbor's dog who was still a puppy and wanted to play like you had so many times before. But you just couldn't. You just looked at us, and we knew it was not going to be possible. I picked you up and carried you the rest of the way home. Your head was down, and life diminished as if the very energy was all but gone. It was so sad. I loved you so much.

At home, I laid you on the couch and sat next to you. You were spent. It was as if you knew time was short, but each moment again was precious and worth the pain. But this time, filled with sadness, and a sense of dread as we now knew fully, time was slipping.

Dear Ed,

I needed to say goodbye in my own way. I was so tired and it was indeed painful to walk, but please don't feel guilty. Those last steps were for both of us. I felt the sadness too. How could I not? The ritual of our walks, and saying goodbye had to have its place. I feel lucky we had that one last time to loop around the neighborhood. Shared loving pain is needed, but so hard to bear.

Dear Peter,

Desperate measures wouldn't help as there was no treatment that money or love could buy. The nodules on your liver were now multiplying and the tumors on your spleen, well, there was nothing we could do.

I had to practice what you had taught me, to live with acceptance.

You stayed curled up next to me, but it felt different, filled instead with the dread of the morning and what it would bring. I know I didn't sleep at all that night, wanting to spend every moment and breath left with you.

As we ventured out into the yard the next morning, the sun made a welcome appearance, peeking out from behind the cold, gray sky. This was the same yard where we had shared countless moments. You had always adored lounging in the grass, taking in the scents of the bushes, and investigating the familiar ground. On this day, you gazed around, taking your time, and then turned your attention to the door, a silent indication that you were ready to head back inside.

Then all too soon, there was a knock on the door.

It was time.

We settled you gently on your favorite blue blanket, in your spot on the couch —waiting for us or basking peacefully in the sunlight streaming through the window. We chose this for you, to be comfortable at home with a veterinarian who specialized in at-home end of life care.

Everyone took turns holding you, offering comfort and saying our goodbyes. The thought of letting you go was overwhelming. Even little Judy sensed it as she snuggled up to you and you to her.

You passed away just as you lived - surrounded by the love of those who cherished you. Despite your illness, you held onto your courage and dignity until the end. You were prepared for this moment, just as you lived your life openly and honestly. Your presence allowed us to be with you, even in your suffering. It was your final gift to us.

In your last moments, you exhibited a sense of grace and purity that seemed impossible, showing us that even in the face of death, there can be acceptance without fear. I'd like to believe that all dogs find their way to a peaceful place, a kind of canine heaven. I hope that you've found that place of rest and joy, and I'll keep you in my prayers, my dear friend. You died 3/5/2019. I will always remember.

Dear Ed,

Each of us will face this moment, over and over again, until it's your turn. Remember now there is more beyond this existence. And I carry you in my soul. The cycle of life is always talked about, but it still comes as a shock. Please know I was ready when my time came. I was in pain.

I know you had me cremated, and it touches my heart that my ashes now rest on your dresser. Your thoughtful gesture of placing my name plaque in the backyard, next to the rose bush, means a lot to me as well.

Things could have been so different. Some never find a place filled with love and warmth like I did. I cherished you all.

Dear Peter,

As you lived, you died. Surrounded by love. Your dignity, and courage were there even when you were so sick. You were ready. You faced that too as you lived your life, openly and honestly. You gave us the chance to be with you. It was your last gift to us, even as you suffered. You had a sense of grace and purity at such a time when it seemed impossible. You showed us that death need not be feared, but to accept that it has its own inevitable place. Hopefully, the way of your passing provided you peace. I like to believe all dogs go to heaven. If anyone that pure does not, then there seems little chance us humans have the qualities to seek such a place. Someone as good and kind as you must have a place of rest and joy. I pray that is so.

We miss you each day.

CLOSING THOUGHTS

Time – there is never enough

As I sit here at age 69, I wonder where the time went. I know it's a cliché, but it's true. The time given to us is never enough.

I'd like to think we never took all those wonderful days of playing, laying around, and sharing all that we could for granted. But we did. Each in our own ways. We could have taken Peter on more car rides, spent a little longer outside in the sun he loved so much, and played with him just a little bit longer. Each moment counted. That's why death is shocking, even when it's expected. It means there's no more time left to go back into the relationship.

We have our family, our children, our precious grand-children, and some good friends who all bring something special to our lives. It's so easy to say no to things, especially when life gets busy and exhausting. We're not getting any younger, and we know our time is running out too. The lesson that time is short, and we should make the most of the moments we have, can't be said enough.

If a little white dog could live life so well, surely we can too. I'll do my best to do it even better.

Dear Peter,

I have a strong science background. I read a lot. Linda sometimes tells me I think too much. I'm pretty rational about most things. But once again, you Peter, have made me rethink those things I thought I knew so well.

Strange things have happened since you died. I will think of you as I lie in bed and how it felt when you laid next to me all night long for so many years. Other than my wife, I know I've spent more hours with you than any other living being on this planet. Your curling up next to me, finding your spot in the crook of my legs made sleep easy. As odd as it sounds, I often felt you next to me months after you were gone. Linda also felt you in the room, doing your circles to settle down before finally curling up next to us, just like you used to.

While I want you to be at peace and settled, a part of me really hopes your spirit is still around, and sharing with us whatever part of you is possible. I don't know if others have had similar feelings or experiences, but I don't care. I'm glad we do.

Thank you for coming into our lives. Perhaps this poem can share something that illustrated these feelings that occurred. Once again, I think a dog seems to be better able to show this than most of us humans.

SEARCHING

We grieve that Jane's away
I know she's dead – but Gus is
Never so sure. Today
*   He mopes and fusses.*

And when we're back from walking
He sniffs at her armchair
And listens for her talking,
*   And climbs the stair*

To poke an inquiring nose
Under the hamper's lid,
For Jane, he must suppose,
*   Returned and hid.*

Donald Hall, (2011), Searching, in The Back Chamber, Houghton Mifflin Harcourt

Dear Readers:

The first draft of this book was written to help deal with the feelings of loss and grief that I had following Peter's death. It came from trying to make sense of why the feelings were so strong in this relationship when other loved ones, who meant so much to me, didn't find expression or were experienced in as powerful a way.

It helped after a while to think of the memories as times where something important was gained, if one only listened carefully enough. Then, after writing a very emotional first draft, through tears and pain, I put it away, sort of like a journal, never really intending to share it with anyone other than my wife.

It took a few years for the loss to hurt a bit less. That's when I called up the memories and read the stories again. It still brought strong feelings out, but I was able to read the stories that had just poured out at the time it was roughly drafted.

Having written before, books on psychology, scientific articles and chapters, it seemed natural to take the raw stories, and shape them just a bit more. The day came when others heard mention of what had been written, and I shared the stories with my sons and daughter-in-law. Then Covid hit and the project was shelved again. Until now.

The hope is the stories of our time with Peter will resonate with others. He touched us in ways that when we tell the stories to others, typically dog people, they smile and grow sad with their own stories and memories. People who have never had a dog, and heaven forbid those who said that they never ever wanted to have a dog, have also said they liked the book and were touched by the stories.

As a psychologist, I have discovered that storytelling stands as one of the most powerful ways to gain insight and perspective that can lead to personal development through growth and change when dealing with life events. To this end, knowing Peter as I did, I believe that these are the sentiments he would have expressed if only he could talk.

It is my hope these stories, from the life of a little white dog, are able to help with some of that change in others. If they do, then his life will continue to touch people as he did with ours.

It came to me
that every time
I lose a dog
they take a piece
of my heart with them,
And every new dog
who comes into my life
gifts me with a piece
of their heart.
If I live long enough
all the components
of my heart
will be dog, and
I will become
as generous and
loving as they are.

-anonymous

As cited in, Tom Stella, (2017). With permission. CPR for the Soul: Reviving a Sense of the Sacred in Everyday Life. Woodlake Publishing.

LESSONS FROM PETER

With nearly four decades of experience working as a psychologist, I've had the honor of working with countless numbers of clients as they grappled with events that have brought them immense pain and suffering. In my efforts to console and guide them, I also had the privilege and opportunity to examine the human condition. But somehow, it was you, Peter, who brought those lessons home by observing and learning from you how to become a better, more compassionate human.

And now, I am left to practice all the lessons that are etched in my heart. Here they are:

Unconditional love: You never judged me for my flaws or mistakes. This taught me the importance of offering love and compassion to others without conditions.

Living in the present: You had a remarkable ability to live in the moment. This taught me to appreciate the present and not let past regrets or future anxieties consume me.

Loyalty and commitment: You were incredibly loyal to your first family too. This taught me the importance of nurturing strong, long-lasting relationships with those we care about.

Resilience: You endured physical challenges and set-backs with remarkable resilience as you bounced back and continued to enjoy life. This taught me to face adversity.

Forgiveness: You were always so forgiving of everyone and everything. You never held grudges and readily forgave us, even after being scolded. This taught me to let go of resentment and practice forgiveness in my own life.

Non-Verbal communication: Your body language was tied into your emotions and your emotions to your body language. This taught me to understand and respond to peoples' cues and to be more attuned to non-verbal communication.

Adaptability: You were always game to go anywhere, anytime. This taught me the importance of flexibility and adaptability in a constantly changing world.

Joy in simple things: You always found joy in the simple pleasure of life. This taught me to slow down and find happiness in the small, everyday moments.

Patience: You were always so patient in waiting for a walk or meals as well as for our attention. This taught me the value of waiting and not rushing through life.

Unwavering trust: You trusted me implicitly. This taught me the significance of trust in building strong bonds with others.

Empathy: You had such a keen sense of empathy that you always knew when someone was happy or upset and in need of comfort. This taught me the power of empathy and compassion.

ACKNOWLEDGEMENTS

Few books like this ever gets done without considerable help. First, I'd like to thank the numerous readers who made the first drafts of this so much better. They included (and I hope not to leave any out), Judy, Gayle, Rachel, Patricia and Melanie. Second, I'd like to acknowledge the efforts of Abbie, Linda and Laura, without whom this book would not be anything like it is now.

AUTHOR BIO

Edward Hickling is a licensed psychologist who likes to spend his time with his family, which includes his wife, two sons, two daughters-in-law and two grandchildren. He has written several professional books related to trauma and resilience, including *After the Crash: Assessment and Treatment of Motor Vehicle Accident Survivors; Overcoming the Trauma of Your Motor Vehicle Accident: A Cognitive Behavioral Treatment Program; and Transforming Tragedy: Finding Growth Following Life's Traumas.* Peter was a central part of his life for more than ten years, and found a place in his life unlike any other. Ed now shares his pet life with Riley, another Bichon, who in almost all ways is not like Peter. And that's just fine.

Made in the USA
Middletown, DE
22 July 2024